Six Sonatas

FOR

FLUTE AND PIANO

by

J.S. BACH

Revised by Jean Albert de la Tournerie
and John Wummer

SMC
★
B 433

SOUTHERN MUSIC COMPANY

SONATE I.

J.-S. Bach

FLUTE

Andante. (Allegro moderato.)

B433

PIANO.

Andante. (Allegro moderato.)

SOUTHERN MUSIC COMPANY
SAN ANTONIO, TEXAS 78292

B433

B433

Largo e dolce.

C

D

Allegro (moderato).

Allegro (moderato).

SONATE II.

Bach

FLUTE

Allegro moderato.

PIANO.

Allegro moderato.

A

R433

Siciliano.

Six Sonatas for Flute and Piano

By J. S. BACH

Revised by John Wummer &
Jean Albert de la Tournerie

FLUTE

SONATE I

Andante. (Allegro moderato.)

SOUTHERN MUSIC COMPANY
SAN ANTONIO, TEXAS 78206

4

Largo e dolce.

6

Allegro (moderato).

SONATE II.

Allegro moderato.

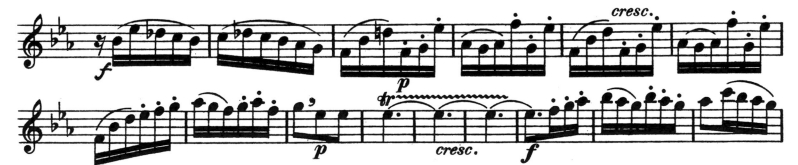

SONATE III.

SONATE IV.

Allegro.

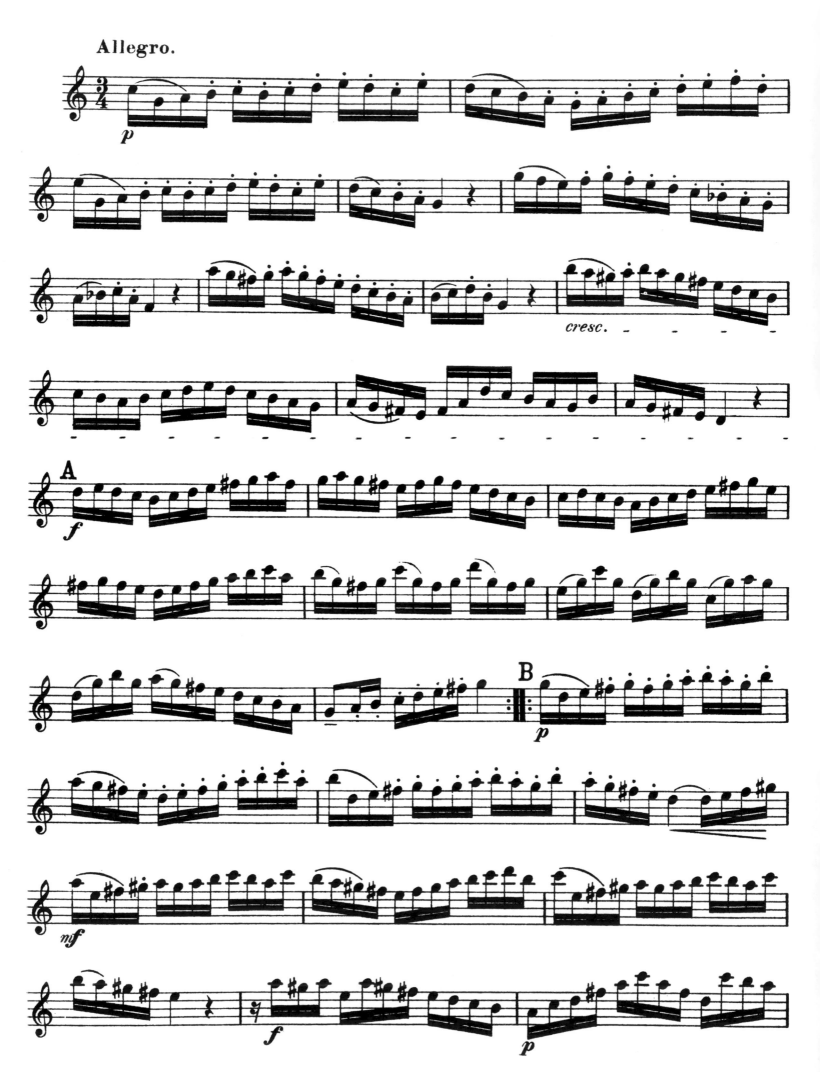

Menuetto I.

dolce

Menuetto II.

cresc.   mf

p

dim.   Menuetto I D.C.

SONATE V

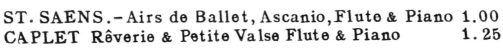

Allegro.

Allegro.

SONATE VI.

Adagio ma non tanto.

Siciliano.

dolce

mf   p

p   dolce

cresc.   f   dol.

poco cresc.   p   2ⁿᵈ time Rall.

Allegro assai.

p   tr

cresc.

Fine.

Selected Flute Publications

COLLECTIONS

BACH, J.S.
Andraud, Albert J.

| B432 | 24 Flute Concert Studies | HL3770628 |

This extraordinary flute repertoire collection is an extraordinary value for the serious flute player/student. In addition to the studies based on the works of J.S. Bach, it includes significant flute repertoire of other major composers (flute solo parts only):

BACH, J.S.
Mols, Robert

| B230 | 20 Concert Studies | HL3770321 |

BENNETT, WILLIAM

| B363 | My Favorite Encores | HL3770551 |

Compiled and arranged by William Bennett.

BIZET, GEORGES
Andraud, Albert J.

| SS380 | Three Pieces | HL3774014 |

DEVIENNE, FRANCOIS
Andraud, Albert J.

| B408 | Six Sonatas | HL3770620 |

DEVIENNE, FRANCOIS
Moskovitz, Harry

| B271 | 24 Progressive Duets | HL3770384 |

These progressively arranged duets start at the advanced beginner level and introduce players to key signatures ranging from three flats to three sharps. They also introduce pieces in compound meters.

DEVIENNE, FRANCOIS
Wienandt, Elwyn

| B239 | 38 Duos for Flutes | HL3770341 |

EPHROSS, ARTHUR
Ephross, Arthur/ Stark, Jan

| B392CO | Church Instrumentalist, Bk. 1a | HL3770593 |

KOEHLER/DROUET

| SS246 | Six Sonatinas and Three Duos Concertants | HL3773854 |

This collection of flute duets includes "Six Sonatinas" Op. 96 by Hans Koehler and "Three Duos Concetants" by LFP Drouet.

LEEUWEN, ARY VAN

| ST195 | Cadenzas for Mozart's G Major Concerto | HL3774794 |

LEHMAN, RALPH
Ephross, Arthur

| B483 | Church Instrumentalist, Bk. 2a (Christmas) | HL3770755 |

MILLS, PATRICIA

| B573 | Famous Flute Works: Anthology of Studies for Flute | HL3770918 |

MOZART, WOLFGANG AMADEUS
Various

| ST987 | Cadenzas for Concerto in G Major | HL3775893 |

TELEMANN, GEORG PHILLIPP
Cole, Robert

| B334 | 12 Fantasies | HL3770501 |

The "Twelve Fantasies" are a faithful reflection of the "gallant style" of the age. They were written about 1732, during the height of Telemann's career and faithfully depict his movement away from the Baroque into freer forms, giving an improvisatory and somewhat spontaneous feeling to these works. Telemann, as was common of his era, did not suggest many dynamic markings or phrasings. In the edition, editor Robert Cole has added metronome markings, slurs, dynamics, and breath markings as he would employ them in performance.

TELEMANN, GEORG PHILLIPP
Ephross, Arthur

| B355 | Fantasies 13- 24 | HL3770541 |

VIVALDI, ANTONIO
Wye, Trevor

| B330CO | Il Pastor Fido (Six Sonatas) | HL3770496 |

This edition has been guided by 18th century practice and style. Research on the pieces contained in this collection has shown that most of these sonatas are probably a pastiche, partly of Vivaldi concerti themes, and partly of works by other composers. This version has both a fully realized piano accompaniment and a continuo part for those who wish the full Baroque experience.

VOXMAN, HIMIE

| B490 | Duet Fun, Bk. 1 | HL3770771 |
| B491 | Duet Fun, Bk. 2 | HL3770772 |

Exclusively distributed by  HAL•LEONARD® CORPORATION

Questions/ comments? info@laurenkeisermusic.com

SONATE III.

Bach

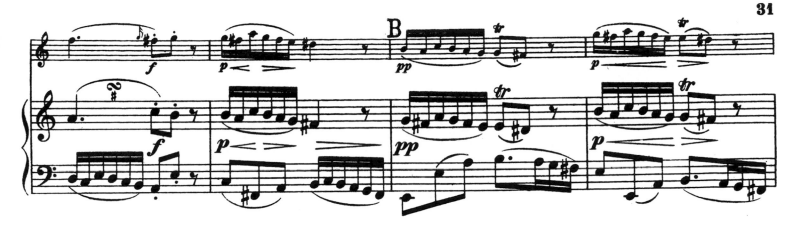

R433

SONATE IV.

Bach

Allegro.

Allegro.

Menuetto II.

Menuetto II.

Menuetto I D.C.

SONATE V.

Bach

FLÛTE

Adagio ma non tanto.

PIANO.

Adagio ma non tanto.

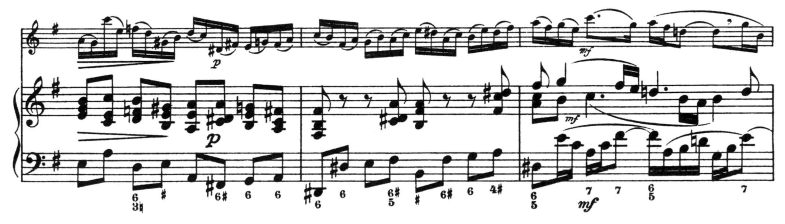

B433

Allegro.

Allegro.

A

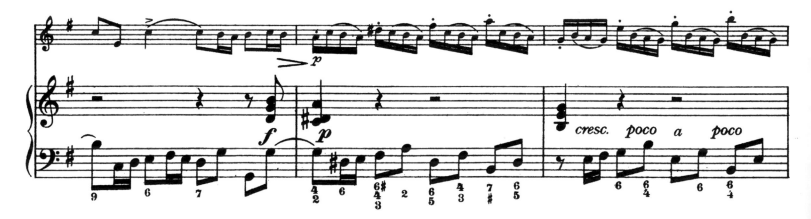

B433

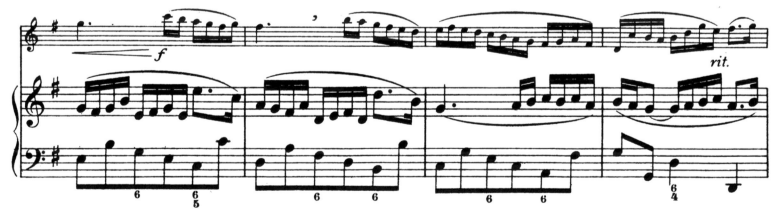

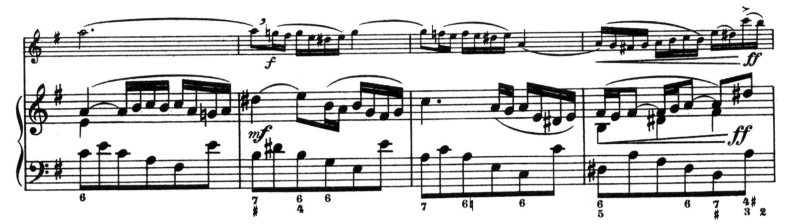

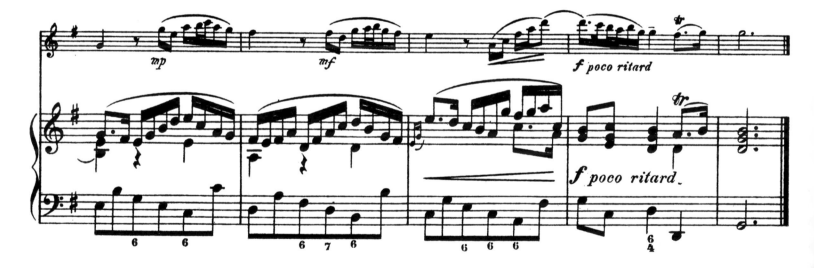

B433

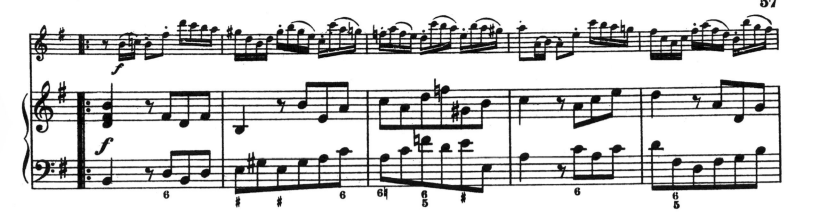

SONATE VI.

Bach

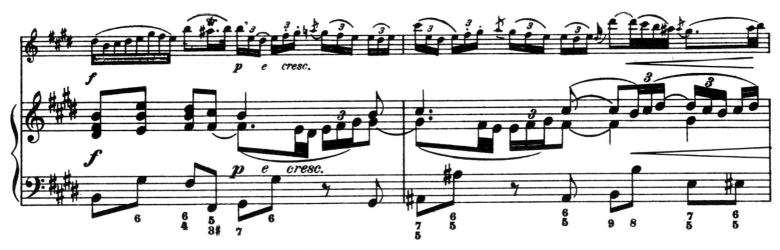

B433

Allegro.

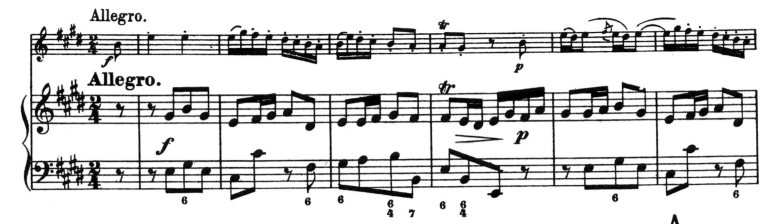

A

B

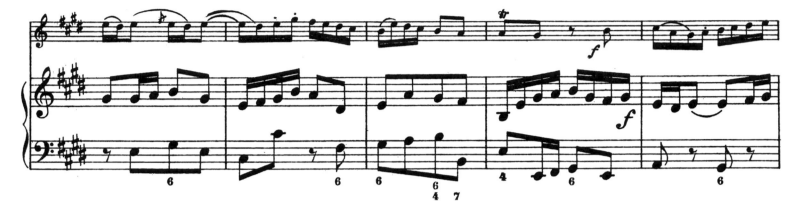

Fine.

SELECTED FLUTE SOLOS AND STUDIES

Flute Etudes and Instruction

ANDERSEN, JOACHIM
ed. Carol Wincenc

S112002   Twenty-Four Etudes for Flute (with Flute 2 part), Op. 15   HL42675

This edition immortalizes Ms. Wincenc's inspiring sessions with the great French flutist Marcel Moyse by creating a second flute part playable by the teacher or a fellow student. This unique approach underscores the musical elements within the lines and teaches the student rhythmic stability, phrasing, intonation, and quality of sound by playing with the master. The edition also offers a unique glimpse into Andersen's brilliance and creativity with the included manuscript fragment and sketch from his Etude Op. 15 Number 1.

BERBIGUIER, BENOIT TRANQUILLE
ed./Fl. 2 by Carol Wincenc

S112003   18 Studies for Flute (Urtext Edition with Flute 2 Part)   HL109366

The 18 studies presented here by Renowned French flutist Benoit Tranquille Berbiguier (1782-1838) are among his most often-played pieces, recognized for their musical as well as pedagogical value, and are an important part of any flutist's training. This is a new Urtext edition with a Flute 2 part composed by Carol Wincenc, based on the methods of one of her most pivotal influences, the great flutist Marcel Moyse.

BERBIGUIER, BENOIT TRANQUILLE
Judith Thomas

B336   18 Exercises   HL3770503

DICK, ROBERT

S110002   The Other Flute Manual   HL40113

An essential reference work of contemporary flute techniques.

S110003   Tone Development Through Extended Techniques   HL40114

Daily studies for developing resonance and the embouchure.

DROUET, JEAN-PIERRE
Arthur Ephross

B499   25 Famous Studies   HL3770822

GILBERT, GEOFFREY

B397   Sequences   HL3770604

B369   Technical Flexibility   HL3770557

KOEHLER, ERNESTO
ed. Carol Wincenc

S110021   35 Exercises for Flute, Op. 33 (Book 1)   HL42282

Newly engraved and formatted with a clean look of this classic flute book with editorial comments and direction by Carol Wincenc.

S110022   35 Exercises for Flute, Op. 33 (Book 2)   HL42283

REICHERT, M.A.
ed. Carol Wincenc

S110020   Seven Daily Exercises, Op. 5   HL42281

The Reichert Seven Daily Exercises (Op. 5) has long been one of the most useful, respected, and treasured learning methods written for the flute. With this new, easier to read edition with the editorial guidance of world-class flutist Carol Wincenc, a new generation of players has access to immeasurable hours of exacting and nuanced instruction, wherever they are in their own development.

VARIOUS
Andraud, Albert

B430   The Modern Flutist   HL3770626

The serious flute player/student will find studies based on thirty of the most standard works of orchestral repertoire as well as the 8 etudes de salon by Donjon and the thirty caprices of Karg-Elert.

Flute Solo, unaccompanied

DICK, ROBERT

S110011   Lookout   HL40129

A tonal, melodic rock solo for flute that uses easy multiphonics.

Flute Solo with Keyboard

BACH, C.P.E.
Arthur Ephross/ Jan Stark/ Richard Thur

ST911   Sonata in G (Hamburg)   HL3775767

BACH, J.S.
Wummer, John

B433CO	Six Sonatas	HL3770630
SS117	Sonata No. 2 in E-flat	HL3773717
SS119	Sonata No. 4 in C	HL3773719
SS120	Sonata No. 5 in E-minor	HL3773721

BOCCHERINI, LUIGI
Ary Van Leeuwen

SS208   Concerto in D Major, Op. 27   HL3773818

CHAMINADE, CECILE

SS212   Concertino   HL3773823

ENESCO, GEORGES

SS216   Cantabile and Presto   HL3773826

EWAZEN, ERIC

SU446   Ballade, Pastorale and Dance   HL3776364

FAURE, GABRIEL-URBAIN
Arthur Ephross

SS828   Fantasie   HL3774493

FOOTE, ARTHUR
Eleanor Zverov

ST83   A Night Piece   HL3775663

GANNE, LOUIS

SS217   Andante and Scherzo   HL3773827

KOEHLER, ERNESTO
Arthur Ephross

SU66   Papillon   HL3776498

MOUQUET, JULES

SS156   La Flute De Pan   HL3773761

MOZART, WOLFGANG AMADEUS
Van Leeuwen

SS234	Concerto in D, K314	HL3773834
SS235	Concerto in G, K313	HL3773835

QUANTZ, JOHANN JOACHIM
Wummer, John

SS238   Concerto in G Major   HL3773840

SAINT SAENS, CAMILLE

SS135   Airs De Ballet D'ascanio   HL3773738

SCHUMANN, ROBERT
Guenther, Ralph

ST478   Three Romances   HL3775176

TAFFANEL, PAUL
Arthur Ephross

ST223   Fantaisie on Themes From Der Freischutz   HL3774836

TAFFANEL, PAUL
Bennett, William I.B.

ST552   Grande Fantaisie on Themes From Mignon By Thomas   HL3775280

TELEMANN, GEORG PHILLIPP
Wummer, John

SS242   Suite in A Minor   HL3773845

WIDOR, CHARLES-MARIE

SS165   Suite   HL3773771

Exclusively distributed by  HAL•LEONARD® CORPORATION

Questions/ comments? info@laurenkeisermusic.com